ANATOMICAL DRAWING OF FLOWERS COLORING BOOK

I0710954

By: Digital Coloring Books

ISBN: 10: 1983543179
ISBN-13: 978-1983543173

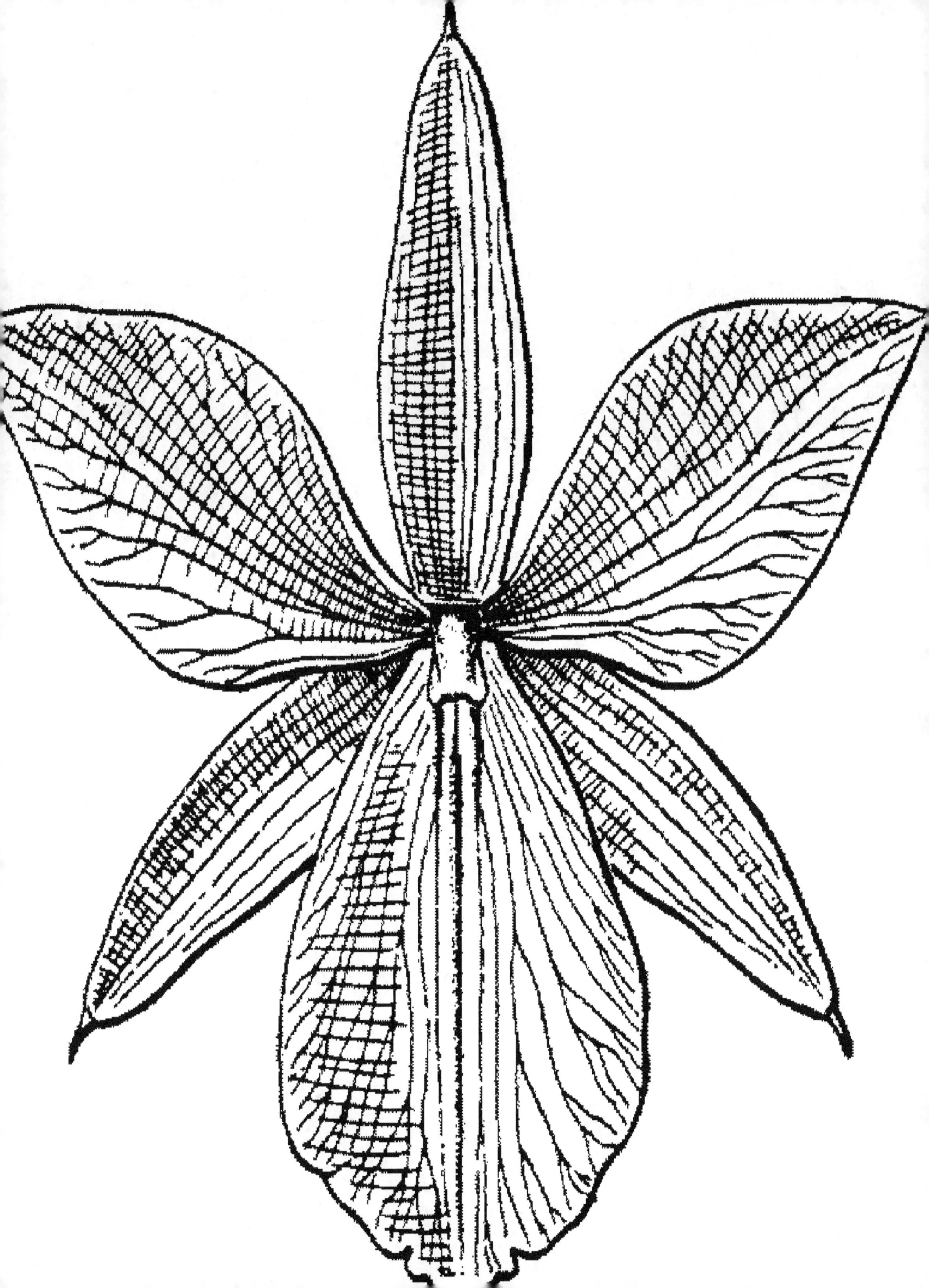

GORDON
Dillon

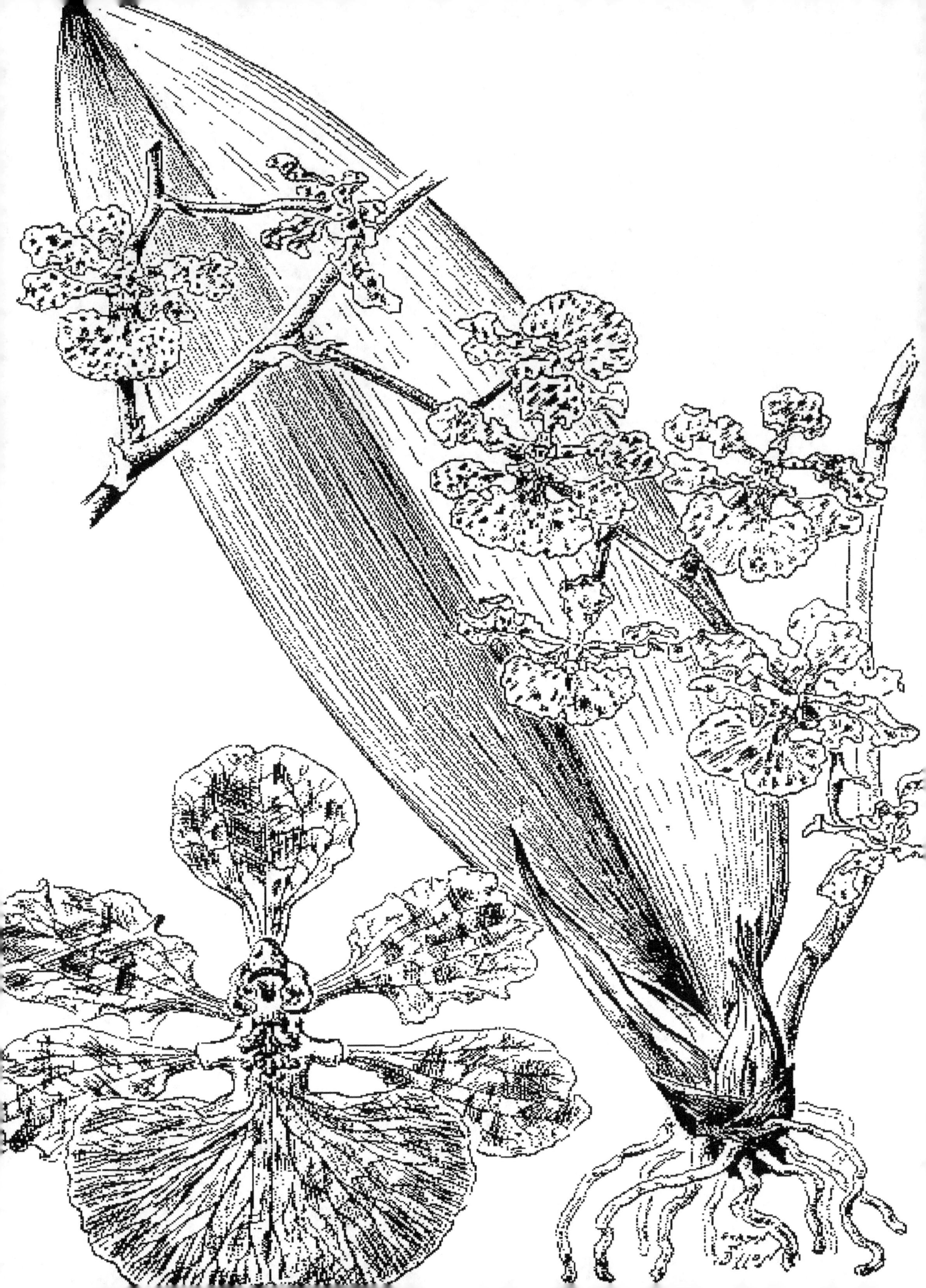

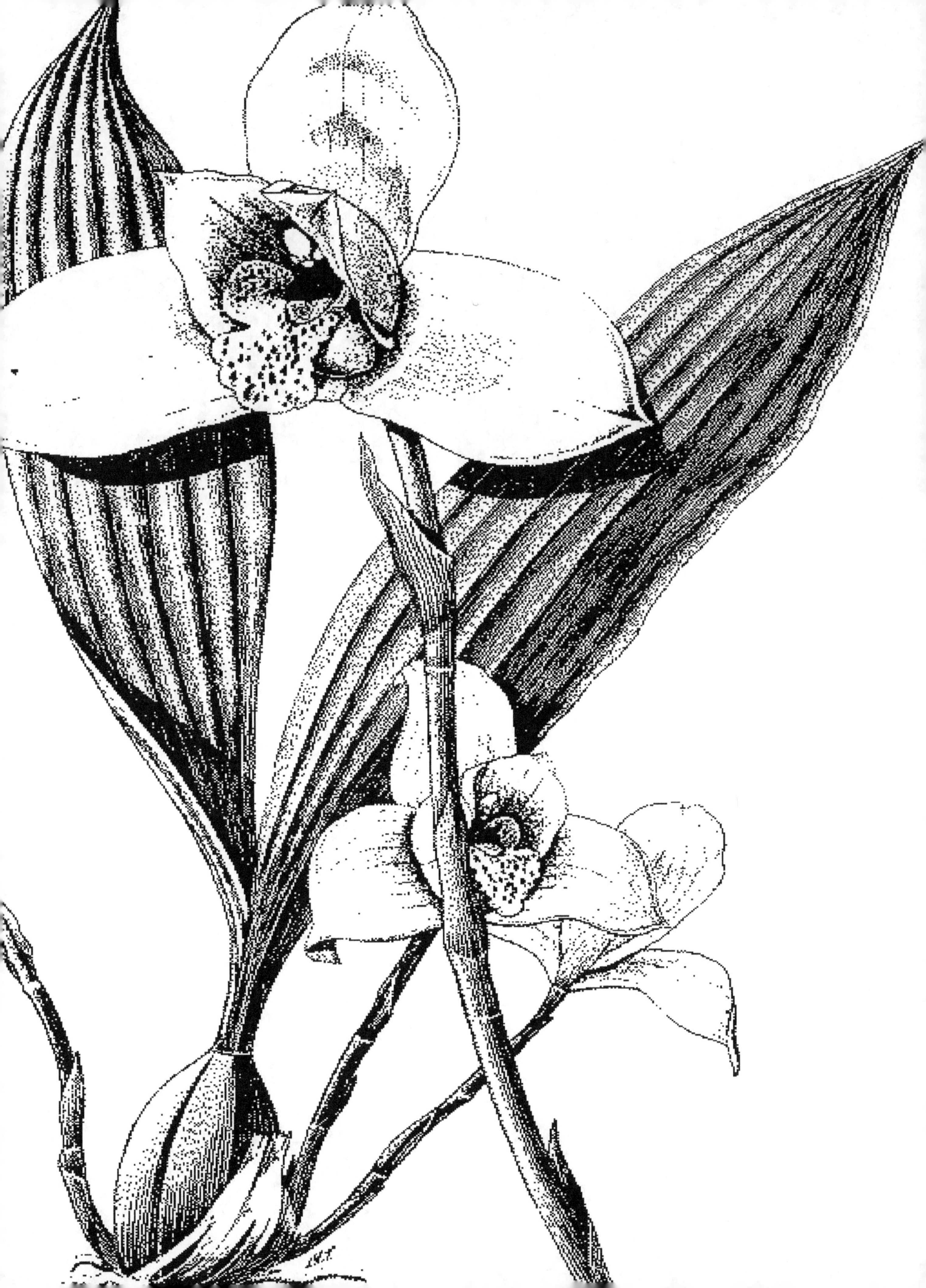

4
GORDON
W.
DILLON

www.ingramcontent.com/pod-product-compliance
Lightning Source LLC
Chambersburg PA
CBHW081325250726
48662CB00008B/2752
* 9 7 8 1 9 8 3 5 4 3 1 7 3 *